To my
sister Elizabeth,

Remember as you read this book, my sister
that there is God above watching
over all that you do and may
you walk in the sunlight
as God shines on you.

Love and
Happy Birthday
Joanne

FOR
ALL THAT
LIVES

*"The basic concept on which goodness rests
is reverence of life—the great mystery in which
we find ourselves with all living things."*

By Ann Atwood
and Erica Anderson

FOR
ALL THAT
LIVES

with the words of
Albert Schweitzer

PUBLISHED BY
CHARLES SCRIBNER'S SONS, NEW YORK

1 3 5 7 9 11 13 15 17 19 PD/C 20 18 16 14 12 10 8 6 4 2
Printed in the United States of America
Library of Congress Catalog Card Number 74-7809
ISBN 0-684-14001-2

ACKNOWLEDGMENTS Grateful acknowledgment is made for permission to reprint the following quotations:

Pages 20 (top), 21, 29 from *The Animal World of Albert Schweitzer*, edited and translated by Charles R. Joy, reprinted with permission of Beacon Press; 16 (top) from *Christianity and the Religions of the World* by Albert Schweitzer, translated by Joanna Powers, reprinted with permission of George Allen & Unwin; 14, 19 (bottom), 23, 27 (bottom), 28 from "Civilization and Ethics," Part II, from *The Philosophy of Civilization* by Albert Schweitzer, translated by C. T. Campion, reprinted with permission of Macmillan Publishing Co., Inc. and Adam and Charles Black, Ltd.; 9, 11, 12 from "The Ethics of Reverence for Life" by Albert Schweitzer, from *Christendom*, Volume I, reprinted with permission of the World Council of Churches; 24 from *Indian Thought and Its Development* by Albert Schweitzer, translated by Mrs. C. E. B. Rossell, reprinted with permission of Beacon Press; 17, 19 (middle), 20 (bottom), 30, 31 32 from *Out of My Life and Thought* by Albert Schweitzer, translated by C. T. Campion, reprinted with permission of Holt, Rinehart & Winston, Inc. and George Allen & Unwin; 22 from "Religion and Modern Civilization" by Albert Schweitzer, from *The Christian Century*, Copyright 1934 Christian Century Foundation, reprinted by permission from the November 27, 1934, issue of *The Christian Century*; 2, 5, 6, 15, 16 (bottom), 19 (top), 25, 27 (top) from *The Schweitzer Album: A Portrait in Words and Pictures* by Erica Anderson, reprinted with permission of Harper & Row, Publishers, Inc. and Adam and Charles Black, Ltd. The Authors and the Publisher also wish to acknowledge *A. Schweitzer, an Anthology*, edited by Charles R. Joy, published by Beacon Press; and Harper & Row, Publishers, Inc. for permission to reproduce the photographs on pages 8-9 and 25 from *The Schweitzer Album: A Portrait in Words and Pictures* by Erica Anderson.

"Never say there is nothing beautiful in the world anymore.
There is always something to make you wonder in
the shape of a tree, the trembling of a leaf."

Albert Schweitzer never lost the feeling of wonder he knew as a boy walking alone in the woods near his village in Upper Alsace. In his solitary encounters with the forest and its creatures, he experienced an intimate unity with nature. He felt in himself the same changes that stirred within the earth as each season altered the tones and textures of the landscape.

He was also agonizingly aware of the conflicts within nature, and he sensed that to affirm the world as it is one must acknowledge the unknowable as well as the known.

"It was to me a special mystery how the raindrop, the snowflake, and the hailstone were formed, and I was hurt that people did not recognize the absolute mystery of nature....Already when I was a child it was clear to me that what we call the force of life remains, according to its own being, inexplicable."

As a youth he sensed an elemental harmony between mystery and knowledge, emotion and reason, and between man and the universe. In his quest for this unity he probed deeply into the religions and the philosophies of the East and the West, and into science and art.

By the age of twenty-one, he had found his place in the cosmic scheme of things. Through profound study and meditation he was convinced that love combined with service is the great unifying Force. He made the decision to pursue his several careers until he was thirty, and then to devote himself in whatever way and whatever place his life could make a difference to the world.

Albert Schweitzer is best remembered as "le grand docteur" who built and maintained his own hospital community in French Equatorial Africa, where he died in 1965 at the age of ninety.

From early morning until after dark he gave of himself as doctor, teacher, builder, and friend to the thousands of people who came to him for help. In the late night hours, his only time for solitude, he studied and wrote. His deep concern was for the crisis that faces mankind today. He saw the widening chasm between man and man, and man and his natural environment.

While working on the volumes of his *Philosophy of Civilization*, he struggled to find a saving concept which would be understandable to every age and every culture. One evening at sunset, on a journey up an African river, the phrase "Reverence for Life" flashed into his mind. He had found the key to a universal ethic by which man, through reverence for his own life and all the life around him, could live in harmony with the world and with himself.   *A.A.*

In these words of Albert Schweitzer, one of the great men of our century gives himself again for all that lives:

If we ask, "What is the immediate fact of my consciousness? What do I really know about myself from childhood to old age?".... we find the simple fact of consciousness is this: I WILL TO LIVE—

Through every stage of life this is the one thing I know about myself.

We cannot explain life. . . .

We don't know how life arose out of chemical materials, nor do we know how many years it took to change dead matter into life.

All that we know is that life is a mystery, and we ought to be filled with awe and reverence for this mystery.

Whence the universe came or whither it is bound, or how it happens
to be at all, knowledge cannot tell me.

Only this: that the will-to-live is present everywhere, even as in me.

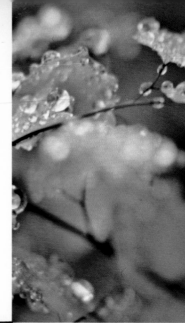

The essential nature of the will-to-live is found in this, that it is determined to live itself out. It bears in itself the impulse to realize itself to the highest perfection.

In delicate blossoms, in the manifold wondrous forms of fishes, in a blade of grass, in the crystal; everywhere it strives to reach that perfection which is implicit in its own nature.

Just as in my own will-to-live there is yearning for more life, and for that mysterious exhaltation of the will-to-live which is called pleasure, and terror in the face of annihilation and injury . . . . which is called pain; so the same obtains in all the will-to-live around me, equally, whether it can express itself to my comprehension or whether it remains unvoiced.

Let us not forget some of the more evolved animals show that they are capable of impressive, sometimes amazing acts of fidelity and devotion.

The deeper we look into nature the more we recognize that it is full of life, and the more profoundly we know that all life is a secret, and we are united to all this life.

We are endowed with the faculty of sharing the lives of other beings, in their joys and fears and grief.

Only in thinking man has the will-to-live become conscious of other will-to-live.

He accepts as being good: to preserve life, to promote life, to raise to its highest value life which is capable of development; and as being evil: to destroy life, to injure life, to repress life which is capable of development.

We have invented many things, but we have not mastered the creation of life. We cannot even create an insect.

We must explain to ourselves and understand that everything that lives is related to us.

A man is ethical only when life, as such, is sacred to him, that of plants and animals as of his fellow men.

A farmer who has mowed down a thousand flowers in his meadow to feed his cows should take care that on the way home he does not, in wanton pastime, switch off the head of a single flower growing at the edge of the road, for in so doing he injures life without being forced to do so by necessity.

The fact that in nature one creature may cause pain to another and even deal with it instinctively in the most cruel way, is a harsh mystery that weighs on us as long as we live.

Creative force does not concern itself about preserving life. One existence holds its own at the cost of another.

We, too, are under the painful law of necessity when, to prolong our own existence, we must bring other creatures to a painful end.
But we should never cease to consider this as something tragic and incomprehensible.

Only so far as a compelling necessity exists for it can we accept the responsibility for the pain and destruction that we ourselves cause living things.

All thinking must renounce the attempt to explain the universe . . . .
The spirit of the universe is at once destructive and creative—it
creates while it destroys, and destroys while it creates . . . .
and we must inevitably resign ourselves to this.

I can do no other than hold on to the fact that the will-to-live appears
in me as the will-to-live which aims at becoming one with other
will-to-live. This fact is the light which shines for me in the darkness.

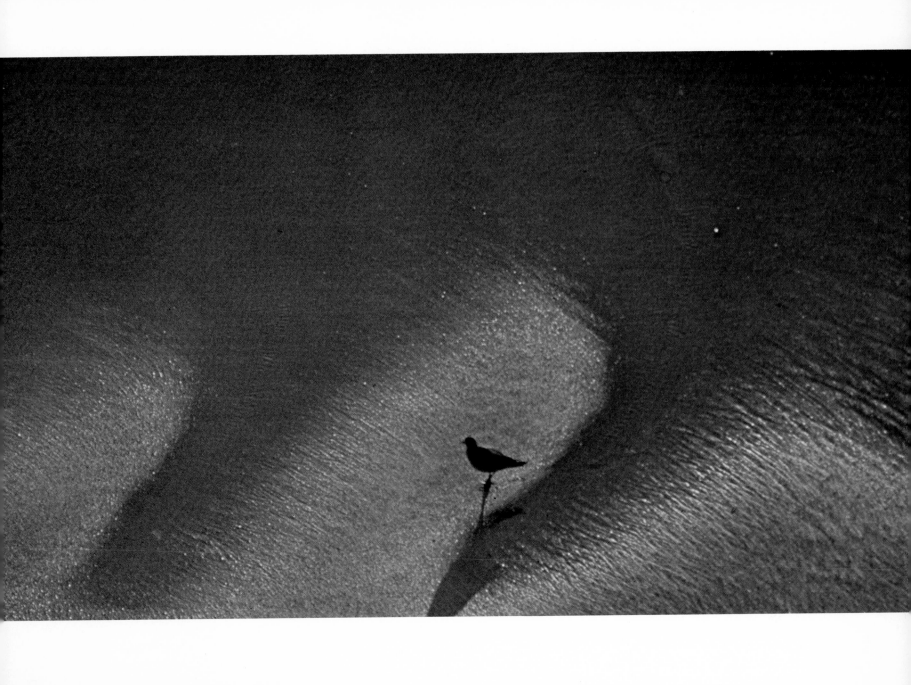

Action directed toward the world is only possible for man in so
far as he strives for the maintenance and furtherance at its highest
level of all life that comes within his range.

We must be men of the future who allow their hearts to speak along
with their reason. Only then we will develop into what we are meant
to be—not supermen—but real men, living and acting in the spirit of
profound humanism.

Formerly people said, Who is
your neighbor?
Man.
Today we know that all living
beings on earth who strive to
maintain life and long to be
spared pain, all living beings are
our neighbors.

*We are like waves that do not move individually, but rise and fall
in rhythm. To share, to rise and fall in rhythm with life around us is
a spiritual necessity.*

*We are born of other lives . . . . we possess the capacity to bring other
lives into existence. So nature compels us to recognize the fact of
mutual dependence, each life necessarily helping the other lives that
are linked to it.*

However much it struggles against it, ethics . . . . must recognize that it can discover no other relationship to other beings as full of sense as the relationship of love.

Love cannot be put under a system of rules and regulations. It issues absolute commands.

Each of us must decide how far he can go toward carrying out the boundless commandments of love without surrendering his own existence. . . .

Let a man begin to think about the mystery of his life and the links which connect him with life that fills the world, and he cannot but bring to bear upon his own life and all other life that comes within his reach the principle of reverence for life.

Existence will thereby become harder for him in every respect than it would be if he lived for himself, but at the same time it will be richer, more beautiful and happier.

It will become, instead of mere living, a real experience of life.

Love is the Eternal Thing which man can already on earth possess as it really is.